BRITAIN IN OLD PHO~~TOGRAPHS~~

BISHOPSTONE & SEAFORD

A Second Selection

PHILIP POPLE &
PATRICIA BERRY

ALAN SUTTON PUBLISHING LIMITED

Alan Sutton Publishing Limited
Phoenix Mill · Far Thrupp · Stroud
Gloucestershire · GL5 2BU

First published 1995

Copyright © Philip Pople and Patricia Berry,
1995

British Library Cataloguing in Publication Data.
A catalogue record for this book is available from
the British Library.

ISBN 0-7509-0928-5

Typeset in 9/10 Sabon.
Typesetting and origination by
Alan Sutton Publishing Limited.
Printed in Great Britain by
WBC Ltd, Bridgend, Mid Glamorgan.

Contents

Bishopstone from Rookery Hill, *c.* 1958. On the left is the new grain building and, in Gratton Field (left foreground), new calf sheds. Within a few years combines would arrive on the scene. The traditional thatched stacks and ricks, seen on the Lower Beacon Fields (behind, left), and those at New Barn (right background), were soon to disappear forever. Above New Barn are the bushes and scrub that formed what was originally called the Bishopstone Cow Down. This open downland space above the farm was used by Sir Thomas Pelham in the mid-seventeenth century for hawking parties. He purchased falcons and goshawks in London and put these birds in mews with those of Sir Edward Burton at Eastbourne. They were then trained by Pelham's friend Nicholas Gildridge. These activities bound the gentry together and even the Civil War was not allowed to interrupt their sport.

Introduction

It is now some four years since we compiled *Bishopstone and Seaford In Old Photographs*. At that time we did not envisage bringing out another selection – fresh pictures, especially of Bishopstone, are scarce. However, we are most grateful to the people who have kindly given or lent material for this book. We have tried to confirm the names of people featured, but memory can fade over the years, and we apologize for errors and omissions.

As we began the second selection it became apparent that we ought to show how differently the two communities developed, yet how they have influenced and supported each other.

An early connection is through Sir Nicholas Pelham, who lived at

Bishopstone Place and defended Seaford against the French in 1545. The greatest link, however, comes during the eighteenth century with Thomas Pelham Holles, first Duke of Newcastle, who also lived at Bishopstone Place. He was a powerful landowner with influence in Seaford and the greater part of east Sussex. He spent much time at his country seat, and a letter from him dated 30 December 1740 to the Duke of Richmond of Goodwood House describes life at Bishopstone.

> My dear Lord, I am very much obliged to you for your kind intention of coming to Bishopstone, but as you can't be with us till Saturday night, and we decamp from hence on Sunday in order to be in London on Monday, I must beg you would not give yourself the trouble to come this time. We had yesterday twice as many people as this house would hold, and all zealous for ye county and most of them so for Lewes also.
>
> We go to Lewes tomorrow, lie there tomorrow night, hunt on Thursday and dine here that day, and shall have a Ball for the Seaford ladies on Thursday night. On Friday we dine at Firle with Sir William Gage and return hither at night, hunt on Saturday and go towards London on Sunday.

In sharp contrast to the duke's idyllic life at Bishopstone was the frenzy of activity on which he embarked in Seaford at election times. The town's age-old involvement with the Cinque Ports system included the right, in return for special maritime services to the sovereign, to return two members to parliament, but electors were restricted to only a few wealthier residents and men of property. The duke had the power to swing the vote in favour of his chosen candidate by putting pressure on the electors, and it is on record that his agents and those of his opponents used bribery and physical force to achieve their ends.

There were 'pocket boroughs' like Seaford throughout the country but, in 1832, the Reform Act swept them away and Seaford lost its political independence, with powerful men like the duke losing their corrupting influence. It should be said that, under the old system, three prime ministers arose directly from Seaford's political associations: the Duke of Newcastle himself, William Pitt the Elder (Earl of Chatham) and George Canning.

Newcastle's private secretary was Thomas Hurdis (1707–84) who, among many other things, was sequestrator at Bishopstone and vicar of Seaford. The benefice of Bishopstone was under sequestration from 1689 to 1844, and was served by various Seaford clergy including Thomas Hurdis junior. The Seaford branch of this family lived in Broad Street; the Bishopstone branch produced James Hurdis, poet and vicar of Bishopstone. Other joint Seaford and Bishopstone clergy were William Snatt, who ended his clerical career by refusing to take the oath to William and Mary, attended two would-be assassins of the king before their execution, and spent some time in Newgate prison; Robert Nowell (1679–89) (dismissed), James Carnegie (1844) and John Harison (1846) from Sutton Place.

Among the more humble families which we find in both communities during the eighteenth century, are those of Medhurst and Allwork. The latter occupied Cleavers and Summer Cottage and also 140 Norton Farm, into which Thomas Allwork moved at Michaelmas 1774. Israel Medhurst, riding officer of the local preventive force (customs men) and landlord of the Duke of Cumberland's Head inn, Lower High Street, lies buried close to the east wall of Seaford parish church.

The 3rd Earl of Chichester, who owned the Bishopstone Estate, provided a school for the village and land for a 150-pupil school in Steyne Road, Seaford.

With the coming of the railway, in 1864, communications improved and cattle for the farms arrived by train to be herded along the road to Bishopstone. Philip Pople's grandfather remembered walking from Norton in 1917 to meet a cockerel off the train. Bishopstone supplied Kennard's dairy with milk and, from 1899 onwards, Seaford with drinking water via Poverty Bottom pumping station.

Until the mid-1950s, Bishopstone and Norton Farms had large workforces. They were housed mainly in tied cottages within the village, but several employees lived in Seaford and would walk across the fields daily, using the footpath that goes in a straight line from the village to Broad Street.

The route we follow in this book is not so direct, but it does in effect lead our readers from the lovely unspoilt village of Bishopstone, through its modern estates to the unique community of Tidemills – now quite lost, but still the subject of many enquiries – and along more than two miles of a seafront that has been the setting for so much dramatic incident and so much leisurely enjoyment, to the startling contrast of Seaford, home to some 22,000 people.

Thomas Pelham Holles (1693–1768) 1st Duke of Newcastle, in Garter robes. Attributed to Charles Jervas. (By courtesy of the National Portrait Gallery, London)

At Bishopstone near to the Sea,
  Upon the Sussex Coast,
As good a Duke as Duke can be
  Lives there – the County's Toast.

His Home and he both open are
  To all that come both near and far.
He has no Private Selfish Ends,
  Esteems his honest Steady Friends.

You ne're can want while he's your Head,
  He gives you Freedom, Meat and Bread.
Your credit nor your Stocks can't fall
  While Pelham represents you all.

Then fill your Glass. Full let it be.
  Newcastle drink while you can see;
With Heart and Voice, all Voters Sing,
  Long live Great Holles – Sussex's King.

Composed by Timothy Goose, a farm servant, Michaelmas, 1741.

VIEWS AND

BUILDINGS

*Bishopstone from the First Plantation, spring
1953. Opposite the stile on the right are the
Shepherds' Steps, which went to the top of Rookery
Hill. One of the last shepherds was Mr Philip
Baker. The Bishopstone flock was sold in 1919;
some of the ewes made £6 each.*

The Manor House, *c.* 1880. This is the earliest photograph so far discovered of this building. The porch is the forerunner of the present one and appears to be made of timber, with an inscription above the door. In those days the post and rail fences were on both sides of the road. This building, along with the rest of the farm and most of the village, was purchased from the Earl of Chichester in September 1912 by Mr Harry Willett for £11,010.

The road in front of the Manor House, *c.* 1947. During the Second World War, British and Canadian troops were stationed in the Manor House. After they left it fell into a state of disrepair, as can be seen from the garden and wall. It made a wonderful place for the village children to play in, until they were found by Mrs Tuckley the headmistress; stories abound!

A drawing of St Andrew's Church, late eighteenth century. This shows the two extra buttresses added to support the sanctuary; just visible is the shuttered Georgian window in the nave. One lancet window can be seen in the choir, the present windows on the south side of the church being inserted or reopened in the 1849 restoration.

The church from the south, c. 1897. Ten children and their teacher from the nearby school stand beside the oak graveboard. These boards were often used as alternatives to headstones, but few survive today. In 1885 the exterior of the church, except the tower, was re-pointed. The work was carried out by the workforce of the Earl of Chichester's estate, responsible for the fabric until 1912.

Interior of the church, eighteenth century. This is the church that the Revd James Hurdis would have known with box pews. The pulpit and sounding-board is on the left. Also visible is the original communion rail, which dates from the time of Archbishop Laud (1573–1645) and is now at the top of the tower, serving as a safety rail. What are now the choir stalls were then the family pews of the principal families; on the left those of Farncombe and Cooper, and on the right those of Pelham and later Catt. In 1736 the Duke of Newcastle applied successfully to Under Sheriff Richard Larder for licence to rebuild his pew.

Interior of the church, c. 1897. After the 1849 restoration the church looked much as it is today, except for the inscriptions of the Lord's Prayer and the Ten Commandments (now painted over) behind the altar. High up in the north wall of the choir are two round-headed Norman windows, blocked up when the north aisle was built in the twelfth century, and discovered during the restoration work.

The church from the lych-gate, *c.* 1934. Iron railings surround the vaults and there is a rather nice gravel path which remained until 1969. The elm trees on the left ran along what was originally the back wall of Bishopstone Place.

The church tower, 1954. Extensive work was undertaken; scaffolding was put up around the entire structure, the roof was reshingled and rotten beams replaced, along with treatment for death watch beetle. The work was done by Braybons of Brighton and cost £551 18s 7d. The tower flintwork is of excellent construction and was originally covered in fine plaster.

The church organ during repair work, *c*. 1955. This instrument was given in 1897 by Mr Harry Willett and his sister Frances Hannah Willett, in memory of Harry's wife Beatrice. Prior to this organ being installed, church music was provided by a barrel organ which stood below the war memorial.

Cleavers, *c*. 1905. Formerly Priory Cottage, this was the home of Samuel Cleaver and John Cleaver the elder and younger, from 1831 to 1895. In due course it was home to Mr and Mrs John Tattersall. He died in 1929, but his wife continued to live here for the next thirty years. Note the bicycle against the wall.

Monksdown, 26 August 1921. Mrs Lishman stands at the front gate of her newly-acquired home. She is the sister of the Misses Fowler who had recently bought the Manor House. Clearly visible is the Victorian glass and cast-iron verandah.

The forge, Silver Lane or Blacksmith Hollow, c. 1925. This building was, for many centuries, a centre of activity within the community: horses were shod, wheels made for carts, farm implements repaired, tools made, to name but a few uses. This building, along with Monksdown (see above), formed part of the Cleavers property, which was by copyhold tenure from the lord of the manor.

Bishopstone from Rookery Hill, *c.* 1938. The church is almost hidden by elm trees and the walled manor garden is full of fruit and vegetables. In the distance are rows of pig houses: large whites were tethered by a long chain and harnesses, while the piglets ran free. The pigs were chiefly the responsibility of Mr Trayt Standen.

Silver Lane, *c.* 1922. On the left is the Great Barn, the granary and Monksdown barn, and the back of the blacksmith's. Monksdown and Cleavers are on the right.

Interior of the Great Barn. This was one of the oldest and largest of the farm buildings. Of medieval origin, it was reconstructed and shortened in the eighteenth century to form a building 26 feet wide and 90 feet long. Regrettably, it was demolished during the 1960s.

View from the top of Silver Lane, 1934. What a wonderful sight: rows of stooks waiting for collection. Beyond are Norton Farm and Peacock Wood on the right, and, in the distance, Beddingham Hill and Firle Beacon.

Bishopstone from Silver Lane. This photograph appeared in the national press during July 1934 together with an article about the sale of the farm to The Guildhall Development Company, which proposed to build some four thousand new homes within the area. The threat of building rumbled on, though it died away during the Second World War. The situation gathered momentum again from 1946 to 1961, but attitudes had changed and everyone was determined to stop development. Petitions were sent to Mr Brook, Minister of Housing. Sir Tufton Beamish, MP for Lewes, visited Bishopstone and was shown around by Mr G.R. Hughes and Mr F.C.H. Fryer, both active members of the Preservation Committee; the Labour MP, Mr Strachey, was also involved. The County Council also discussed the matter at great length and, in the end, compensation and agreement were reached. The land had been saved and reverted to being part of Manor Farm. Locals and visitors alike should never forget how much work and effort were put in to keep Bishopstone as we know it today.

Barrack Cottages and lower part of the Green, *c.* 1935. The Sussex wagon (right) was used as part of the obstacle course in the final event at the village produce shows: the wagon was covered in a tarpaulin sheet, and one had to crawl under it. Beyond the cart originally stood the village pound.

Barrack Cottages, 1910. Word must have spread mighty fast the day the photographer came to take this view. On close inspection nine children can be seen, and someone's mother in the doorway. In the garden are the flint remains of the cottage that once stood on this site. At the end of the Post Office Cottages (right) is a railway carriage, serving as a shed.

Gratton Field, *c.* 1910. Carthorses, foals and calves enjoy the afternoon sunshine. On the left is the cottage which Harry Willett had built four years before this photograph was taken.

Gratton Field with White Row on the left, 1910. On the bottom corner of the green can be seen a horse-drawn delivery van with white canvas top, probably Bannister's, the Newhaven grocer. Also seen is the back of Vine Cottages: it is likely that they were named after John Vine, who was Lord Pelham's steward. John Vine left Pelham's service in 1638 and was rewarded with a parting gift of £40.

Field Cottages, *c*. 1920. In 1777 these cottages were shown as being leased to Mr Cooper of Norton Farm. Two centuries later they were occupied, for the greater part, by the Ford, Mansbridge and Moore families.

The pond and Lady's Meadow, *c*. 1925. Also in view are two cows from Mr L. Willett's Guernsey dairy herd. In days gone by the ponds were dredged with a wooden device pulled from side to side by horses.

Lady's Meadow, looking towards the Rookery, *c.* 1924. The clump of trees was known as the 'twelve apostles'. The trees gradually died or blew down and many of the stumps and roots were blown out by the Laughlin brothers and their supply of explosives (see page 24).

The village and the road to Norton, *c.* 1918. How different things are today, with the field in the foreground occupied by New Cottages, the pick-your-own fruit farm and the greater part of the farm buildings.

New Cottages, summer 1934. It must have been a warm day, as Philip's grandmother, Mrs F.M. Pople, has most of the windows open. The cottages had been built in 1924 and cost £1,350. In the distance can be seen George Hughes's new house, Plummers, being built, with the scaffolding around it.

A gentleman sketching at Norton, 1924. He is seated on the lower slope of the hill (known for generations as the Cricket Bat), looking across Ham Lane towards the First and Second Plantations. This photograph was recently found in the north of Scotland.

The waterworks with Waterworks Valley beyond, 1947. It was a daily task, before the days of automation, for Mr F.W. Laughlin (father and son: see page 24) to climb to the top of this hill and sit in a small dug-out with a telescope to read the gauge on the Blatchington reservoir. Thus they knew when to stop pumping.

Steam engines at the waterworks. These engines were installed in 1899 and were working by the summer of 1900. They were supplied by Warner and Company, of Southend, and consisted of two sets of compound condensing steam engines with Cornish boilers and three throw pumps. They cost £4,239.

EVENTS AND PEOPLE

*John Collinson with his nanny, Norton Farm, September
1922. Nanny was Miss May Godley, later Mrs May
Thorpe. She continued to live at Norton until her death in
1989, aged 91. The Collinson family have farmed at
Norton since the early 1920s.*

Bishopstone School, 1917–18. Back row, left to right: Miss Belaires (teacher), ?, Raymond Green, Edith Hopkins, Anne Elliot, Win Elliot, ?, Fred Larkin, Phyllis Burcham, Miss Bloomfield (teacher). Second row: -?-, Jack Geering, ? Churchill (his father was butler at Little Hallands), -?-, ? Pelling, Frank Geering, Joe Geering. Third row: Ted Pook, Len Geering, ? Higgins, Beattie Mansbridge, Lottie Geering, ? Higgins, ? Mockford, ? Higgins, ? Gates. Front row: Horace Crowhurst, Bert Mockford, Tom Mansbridge, -?-, Harry Green, -?- (from Norton), -?- (from Foxhole).

Silver wedding of Mr and Mrs F.W. Laughlin, the Waterworks, 1923. Back row, left to right: their four sons, Percy, George, Fred, Phil. Front row: their daughter Nancy, Ruth and William (Mr and Mrs F.W. Laughlin), their daughter-in-law Lila (wife of Phil) and their first grandson John Laughlin. The Laughlin family lived at the Waterworks from 1899 to 1966.

BISHOPSTONE.

Post Town, Lewes

Population—300.

A parish between Seaford and Newhaven, can be approached from Claremont road or by footpath across fields from Belgrave road.

Parish Church, Bishopstone—Services. Sundays 11 and 6.30; Second Sunday in the month at 3 p.m. for young people. Holy Communion on first Sunday in month after morning service; on third Sunday after evening service, and on the last Sunday at 8 a.m. Baptisms at 4 p.m. on second Sunday in the month; Service, with Holy Communion, Holy Days and Prayers on Saints Days. Rev. Creswell Roberts (B.A.), Vicar.

Tide Mill Mission Room—Services, Sunday, 3 p.m. Every Tuesday, October to May, 7 p.m.

Stationmaster—Bone, F. J.

Post Office, Bishopstone—Dispatches at 5.55 p.m. Sundays, 5 p.m.

Station Wall B x,5.30 a.m.; 4.30 p m.

Deliveries (through Lewes), 6.30 a.m. and 4.30 p.m. No delivery on Sundays.

Sub-Postmaster, Mr. J. Simmonds.

BISHOPSTONE.

Post Town—Lewes.

Akehurst, Frank (Foxhole)
Bartholomew, Thomas Frederick
Bone, Frederick James, stationmstr.
Burtenshaw, Harry
Clay, E. Nortons cottages
Coleman, Frederick (The Barracks)
Cooper, Allan (Morton Farm)
Cooper, Miss Fanny (Foxhole)
Costobadie, Mrs. (Manor Cottage)
Delves, Edward, Post Office cottages

Durrant, Walter
Elliott, Alfred
Ford, Joseph, Nortons cottages
Ford, Thomas (Rose Cottage)
Green, Robert, Nortons cottages
Hollands, Alfred
Hughes, E. J. blacksmith
Laughlan, William, Waterworks cots
Lester, W. N. Esq. (Marksdown)
Lewis, E. J. Esq. (The Downs)
Longden, Capt. Wilfrid (The Cottage)
M .eDerm .t, Miss (The Priory)
Mockford, Joseph
Mockford, Thomas, Nortons cottages
Moore, David
Parks, Alfred, Nortons cottages
Parks, Nicholas, Nortons cottages
Parsons, Harry (The Barracks)
Pelham, Frederick (Rose Cottage)
Ping, Miss (Ragalug)
Roberts, Rev. Creswell (B.A.) (The Vicarage)
Rush, Miss (Ragalug)
Russell, Edward, Nortons cottages
Simmonds, J. grocer (Post Office)
Stace, Frederick
Tuppen, Thomas, Post Office cottages
Venus, Thomas (Buckle Inn)
Wilkins, Edwin
Willett, Harry (Manor Farm)
Winter, Charles, The Barracks
Witt, Miss, mistress of school (mixed)

BISHOPSTONE ROAD.

Belgrave Road to Bishopstone.

(Rougemont Cottage) Lee, John Wm.

BLATCHINGTON ROAD.

From Claremont Road

(Left from Claremont Road)

1 (Airedale) Wilkinson, W. builder
3 (Twyne Cottage) Court, Lewis
5 (Twyne House) Johnson, Henry
7 Mussell, A. G. fly proprietor
9 Grammer, William
11 **MORLING'S builders' yard and office**
13 Morling, John R.
15 Streeter, Charley

Extract from street directory, 1912. It is self-explanatory, except for the house name of Ragulug; which that was we know not. Only the descendants of Thomas Tuppen and William Laughlin remain resident in the village and at Norton today.

Early Darracq car, *c.* 1923. It had been used by the Laughlin brothers as a taxi at Seaford and Newhaven stations. Taxi-driving did not pay, so they cut the back of the car off, and converted it into a lorry. Mrs Maud Laughlin (left, wife of Fred) and her sister are seated in the cab. On the side is a board which reads 'G. Laughlin. Bishopstone. Seaford'.

Church fête, 11 July 1928. The fête was held annually in the garden of the vicarage, now Bishopstone House. Stella Heaton and John Willett are seen here on the front lawn.

Denis Mackail outside Bishopstone House, *c.* 1937. He was the author of over twenty-five books including a biography of J.M. Barrie, who wrote the play *Peter Pan*. Mackail was the son of Professor John Mackail OM, a grandson of Sir Edward Burne-Jones and brother of the novelist Angela Thirkell (see page 42).

The remarkable Bishopstone tapestry was worked by Mrs Simpson of Watland Furlong, Bishopstone, between 1947 and 1948. Worked in wool, it shows every house and most farm buildings down to the smallest detail, including the oil tanks which stood near the church during the war years. Mrs Simpson was an artist whose work attained professional standard. She died in 1969 in her 101st year.

Bishopstone school, *c.* 1924. This group, in the boys' playground, includes Ted Pook, Lionel Baker, Fred Westwood, Raymond Green, Len Geering, Johnny Gutsell, Charlie Tuppen, Fred Saunders, Tom Westwood and Fred Larkin (see pages 24 and 69).

The Manor House, August 1926. Peggy Thomas and Stella Heaton are in a hammock on the front lawn.

Afternoon tea in the walled manor garden, June 1927. Left to right: Mrs Lishman's knees, the Misses Annie and Maud Fowler, two Inglis boys, Stella and Gladys Heaton. The Misses Fowler bought the Manor House in 1921 and lived there until 1929.

Afternoon tea, 2 New Cottages, July 1946. Left to right: Mr Derek Thacker (elder son of Judge Ransley Thacker KC), Miss Christine Pople (who later married Derek and became Mrs D.R. Thacker), Mrs Winnie Pople, her husband Frank (secretary to Lionel Willett), and their son Colin (who had just returned from active service in India).

Miss Marjorie Mould, September 1933. Miss Mould is sitting on the stile at the bottom of the Shepherds' Steps. In those days the trees in the Rookery had not met up with the first plantation. Dotted around in Ham Lane Field are various pig houses.

125 Vine Cottages, September 1933. While on holiday in Seaford Miss Marjorie Mould (left), Miss Ellen Mould (centre) and Miss Twelvetrees took walks to Bishopstone. They are seen here partaking of tea in the garden of Mr and Mrs Gar Cross's house, 125 Vine Cottages. In the years before the Second World War, tea and cakes could be obtained here during the summer months. In latter years the post office also served teas.

Canadian troops, 24 Bishopstone Road, 1941 or 1942. Most of the bungalows were requisitioned for troops at some time. Out of the 153 men occupying the bungalows only three returned from the Dieppe raid in June 1942.

Monthly meeting of Bishopstone Women's Institute, 8 October 1949. Back row, left to right: Mrs D. Hunt, Mrs Birch, Mrs I.E. Pople, Mrs F.R. Laughlin, -?-, Miss E.M. Keeley, Mrs Cross, -?-, Miss Ridge, Mrs L. Tattersall, Mrs O'Gara, -?-. Front row: Mrs Simpson, Miss Ridge, Miss Molly Simpson, Mrs Jones, Mrs Wadeson, Mrs Price, Mrs Brook, Mrs Burcham.

Bishopstone WI produce show, September 1957. Silver and gold star winners, left to right: Miss Nancy Laughlin, Mrs Maud Laughlin (see page 26), Mrs Brook, -?-, Mrs Winnie Hunt, Mrs Birch, Mrs Mitchell.

Bishopstone WI produce show, 1958. Winners, left to right: Mrs W. Hunt, Mrs Rook, -?-, Mrs Birch, Mrs Joan Willett, Mrs Maud Laughlin.

137 Field Cottages, *c.* 1937. On the annual visit of bed-ridden Aunt Lucy, the Moore family of 137 Field Cottages were joined by the Moores of 142 Norton Farm. Back row, left to right: Don, George, Bessie, Monica, Ethel, Jean, Winnie, Denny, Stephen. Front row: Joseph, Gladys with Bob, -?-, Aunt Lucy in the day bed, the ambulance driver.

Bishopstone, early 1940s. Gathered together are, back row, left to right: Floss Bush, Joyce Bush, Monica Moore, Ethel Moore, Jean Moore, Charlie Tuppen. Front row: Olive Bush, Sheila Frost, Eileen Frost, Margaret Cox.

Norton farm workers, *c.* 1948. Having lunch against the back fence of Watland Furlong are, left to right: Clem Butler, Charlie Butler, Jack Saunders, Tom Burcham, -?-, 'Smokie' Everest (see next page), Fred Trigwell, Jim Smith, Tom Gibbs, Raymond Green, Jack Gutsell.

Bishopstone church path, 10 April 1948. Mr and Mrs Fred Collinson and Mr John Collinson (right) are walking to the church for the wedding of Mr and Mrs Bill Laws. Of all the stories about Norton Farm, the one we like best is about the time when Fred Collinson's car broke down. The nearest garage was at Seaford and, somehow, the car had to be taken there. Not to be beaten, he harnessed a horse to the front of the car, opened the windscreen and put the reins through into the car. Thus they made their way to French's garage (see page 96). Can you imagine doing such a thing today?

Barrack Cottage, *c.* 1954. Standing, left to right: Andrew Woolmer, Jennifer Standen. Back row: Derek Pullen, Ronald Giles, Jennifer Pratt, Rosemary Stevens, Suzanne Everest. Front row: Peter Giles, Judith Pratt, Ian Everest, Linda Pratt.

Presentation of the cup, early 1950s. The Bishopstone team won this competition whose name is now forgotten. Left to right: Johnny Russell, Ralph Foxwell, Bob Moore, Tom Foxwell, 'Smokie' Everest (see previous page), 'Bunny' Moon, Peter Matthews, -?-, 'Roly' Buck with the cup, Jim Morgan, -?-, Peter Hall.

Bishopstone football team, early 1950s. Back row, left to right: Lou Beach, Johnny Russell, Ralph Foxwell, Josh Giles, John Willett, Trayt Standen with Scamp, Peter Matthews, 'Bunny' Moon, Jim Morgan, Harry Cox. Middle row: Bob Moore, 'Smokie' Everest, 'Roly' Buck, Frank Winser. Front row: Tom Foxwell, Johnny Lovegrove, Peter Hall. The mascot holding the ball is Terry Winser.

Social club outing to Southsea, summer 1948. Standing outside the Plough and Sail public house, Crossbush, Arundel, are, back row, left to right: -?-, Pat Matthews, David Westwood, Eileen Saunders, Perce Brook, David Brook, -?-, Billy Beard, John French, Eileen Cox, Bob Procter, Barbara Gutsell, Joyce Honeywood, -?-, Bob Moore. Front row: Billy Beard senior, -?-, Peter Honeywood, Wally Pannel (holding the child), Sid Cox.

Gratton Field, Coronation day, 2 June 1953. The football team are in fancy dress and are, back row, left to right: Ralph Foxwell, Tom Foxwell, Peter Hayward, -?-, John Willett, John Mossop, Jim Morgan, Jack Saunders, Bill Laws, Bob Moore, -?-. Front row: Trayt Standen (in the baby's bath), 'Roly' Buck, 'Smokie' Everest.

Coronation day, 2 June 1953. Among those taking part in the celebrations in Gratton Field are, on the left 'Roly' Buck (dressed as a schoolmaster), Trayt Standen (bottom left), Eileen and Joyce Saunders and, on the right, 'Smokie' Everest (dressed as a nurse).

St Andrew's-tide fair, in the village hall, Wednesday 20 November 1957. At this event are Mrs F.M. Pople and Miss Nancy Laughlin (see page 24), the church organist, with their hardware stall. Most of the items had been acquired by courtesy of the village shop. The fair was opened by Mrs 'Vicar' White at 3 pm and raised £140.

On the fancy goods stall are, left to right: Eric Whitehorn (churchwarden), Frank Pople (Parochial Church Council treasurer), Jack Swan (verger), George Laughlin (churchwarden 1944–59) (see page 24).

LITTLE HALLANDS –
A COUNTRY HOUSE

Little Hallands was occupied by many a distinguished family

from 1900 until 1956. It was purchased in 1924 by

Mr F.D. Pirie and used by him and Sir Adrian and the

Hon. Lady Pollock as a country home. Here the Hon. Lady

Pollock and her youngest grandson, Adrian James McConnel,

are seated in front of the house in 1946.

Little Hallands, late 1940s. It was originally home to the Hurdis family and, from the 1890s to 1907, of Dr W.G. Rutherford, headmaster of Westminster School. From 1907 until 1924 a succession of families occupied the house, including Mr and Mrs Walter Ward, a retired tea planter, and his wife. It was during their time that Emily Davison, the suffragette, was hidden here. Sir Edward Carson had the house for one year; next came Sir Francis Stewart (a servant of the Crown in India) and Lady Stewart, and finally Lord Courthope for nine months, until 1924.

Sutton Place, Seaford, 1902. Frank Pirie, the Hon. Lady Pollock and her daughters, Anne and Betty are seated in this splendid car. Sutton Place was the home of the Hon. Lady Pollock's parents, Viscount and Viscountess Selby. Viscount Selby was formerly William Court Gully, Speaker to the House of Commons from 1895 to 1905. Sutton Place is now part of Newlands School.

Sir Adrian Pollock and his youngest grandson, Adrian James McConnel (see page 39), beside the walnut tree at Little Hallands, 1934. Sir Adrian came from a very distinguished legal family. He was chamberlain of the City of London from 1912 to 1943. Knighted in 1921, he was made a KCMG in 1938 in recognition of his work with visiting foreign dignitaries at the Guildhall.

The Hon. Lady Pollock on the front lawn, *c.* 1944. In front of the house are the blast walls that were built at the beginning of the Second World War by Pettitts, builders from Seaford, to protect the windows in case of bomb damage. The walls were removed in 1945. Pettitts also built an air-raid shelter in the field.

Sir Cyril Asquith in High Court judge's robes, *c.* 1938. The fourth son of H.H. Asquith, the Liberal prime minister, he married Anne Pollock, elder daughter of Sir Adrian and the Hon. Lady Pollock. Educated at Winchester and Balliol, he was called to the Bar, became a High Court judge and was, in due course, made a Lord of Appeal in Ordinary, taking the title Baron Asquith of Bishopstone. In 1951 he was asked by Winston Churchill to become Lord Chancellor, but declined. He died in 1954 and is buried at Bishopstone.

Three of Lord Selby's granddaughters, *c.* 1906. All three girls lived at Bishopstone at some time during their lives. Left to right: Anne Pollock (later Lady Asquith), Diana Grannet (daughter of Sir Guy and Lady Grannet, later Mrs Denis Mackail – see page 27) and Elizabeth Pollock (later Mrs McConnel, the actress and mimic).

Actor/manager Sir Gerald du Maurier, Norton, mid-1920s. He was one of many celebrities who stayed at Little Hallands, including Daphne du Maurier, Cathleen Nesbitt, Noël Coward and Gracie Fields. All were friends of Elizabeth Pollock, who had made her début during the First World War in du Maurier's production of Barrie's *A Kiss for Cinderella*. She appeared in various du Maurier and Coward plays until 1931, when she had the opportunity to produce her own programme of impersonations at the Ambassadors Theatre in London. The victims of her mimicry were various leading ladies.

Outside Little Hallands, *c.* 1946. Setting off for London in the Rover are F.D. Pirie, the Hon. Lady Pollock and George Laughlin, their chauffeur (see pages 24, 26 and 38).

A shopping trip to Seaford, *c.* 1947. Left to right: F.D. Pirie, the Hon. Luke Asquith, the Hon. Jane Asquith, the Hon. Lady Pollock, Betty McConnel (Elizabeth Pollock).

The Rover (left) and the Morris 14 hp outside Little Hallands, *c.* 1947. During the winter of 1947 the Morris almost got stuck in a snowdrift beside Watland Furlong and left the imprint of its number plate in the snow. Gladys Laughlin was driving; her father, George, pushed!

Little Hallands, 1947. Standing just inside the front gate, with the rose garden beyond, are three of the maids. Left to right: Mary (housemaid), Ada Winter (housemaid and, later, cook), Mary Artus (parlourmaid).

The courtyard behind the house, spring 1936. This is one of a series of photographs taken for Suttons' seed catalogue. Suttons supplied the seeds and the plants were grown on and planted out. This was in the days when at least six people worked in the gardens.

The kitchen garden, *c.* 1936. The view is from the back door of Rose Cottage during the winter and hand digging is in progress. The garden grew produce for the household both here and in London. At the far end hens and ducks were also kept.

The kitchen garden, *c.* 1947. The brick path was laid by Pettitts, during the late 1930s, and edged with box hedges. On the left are asparagus beds, raspberries, onions, greenhouse frames, a potting shed and artichokes. On the right are greens, regale lilies, mixed vegetables, potatoes, gooseberries, red-, white-, and blackcurrants, and flowers for cutting.

The kitchen garden, 1936. The gravel path leads towards the main gate. The garden was acquired by Mrs Walter Ward (see page 40) in stages: she would loan money to Mr Alan Cooper of Norton Farm and, if it were not repaid, she would just take some more land instead. The garden is now Bishopstone Nurseries, and has been run, since the mid-1950s, by Mr and Mrs D.P. Wilson.

Second path on the right, kitchen garden, early 1936. Flanking the path are apple trees: on the left Peasgood Nonsuch, Worcester Permain and Lady Sudeley; on the right, Charles Ross, James Grieve, Beauty of Bath and Irish Peach.

Chauffeur's flat with garages, *c.* 1937. Below the flat were, left to right: the workshop, the battery room (which housed rows of batteries in large glass containers), and the garage. The latter had a pit and also housed the paraffin engine which produced the electricity for the house and cottages.

The tennis court, late 1920s. Mr Percy Laughlin (see page 24) and Mr Bill Hampton are at work on the court. Behind them is the playroom, which had formerly been the laundry room.

IN AND AROUND
THE FARMS

*Mr Tom Mansbridge, c. 1945. He is thatching a rick at
Manor Farm, Bishopstone, where he was employed as a
thatcher for over forty years. Before this he worked at
Swanborough Farm and Toye Farm, Firle, and was
probably one of the last bullock-team drivers. He came to
Bishopstone in 1914 and his remarkable work as a
thatcher was known throughout the county. He died in
1957 in his seventieth year.*

Four yoke of oxen, 1898. They are pulling rollers where Manor Farm grain buildings now stand. Beacon Hill is in the background. This and the following two photographs appeared in *Country Life Illustrated* on 26 November 1898.

Mr Harry Willett's oxen, 1898. They are harrowing at Manor Farm, Bishopstone. New Barn is in the distance.

After harrowing, 1898. Barrack Cottages are in the background. These are Welsh black oxen, extremely tough beasts. They would be driven from Wales in large numbers and sold off en route, until the drovers and their remaining animals reached south-east England.

Manor Farm cattle yard, September 1933. Calves enjoy the sunshine in the yard beside Barrack Cottages.

Horse-drawn water carrier, September 1933. While walking to Bishopstone from Seaford Miss Marjorie Mould (see page 30) and her family met the horse-drawn water tanker crossing Whitegate Field. The tanker was part of the steam engine and threshing outfit, as well as being used for various jobs in and around the farm until the early 1960s.

Rookery Field, *c.* 1925. On a hot summer's day, cattle shelter under the trees at the end of the school house garden, with the rookery in the distance. Two hens scratch around, to complete the scene.

Manor Farm, *c.* 1953. Mr Louis Suitter thatches a rick on the farm. New Barn Road is in the distance.

Inces Barn, Norton Farm, 1930. The barn provided much talk at the time, for it caught fire on Easter Day, 1930. Fred Collinson and Frank Grantham are surveying the wreckage.

The other end of the barn, with all sorts of burnt-out farm machinery and charred timbers.

Arthur Ford with auto plough, late 1920s. The inventor was one of the five sons of Thomas and Mary Ford of 137 Field Cottages, and the father of Professor Sir Hugh Ford FRS.

Norton Farm workforce, late 1940s. They are threshing a stack at Cut Hole, between Foxhole Farm and Mount Pleasant.

Harvesting, Norton Farm, 1940s. Fred Trigwell is on the binder, and 'Smokie' Everest driving the tractor (see page 34).

Harvesting, Manor Farm, Bishopstone, *c.* 1951. 'Smokie' Everest is on the binder with Perce Brook driving the tractor.

Norton Farm, late 1940s. The Fordson Major tractor, with elevator, stands by two ricks.

Norton Farm, autumn 1948. Among those helping to build the corn stack are Bill Gibbs, Peter Hayward and Fred Trigwell.

Threshing at Norton Farm, winter 1948. In the field adjoining Little Hallands, and so known as 'Pirie's', at the end of the kitchen garden, threshing goes on amid clouds of dust.

Norton Farm, winter 1948. Among the threshing gang are Jim Smith, Fred Trigwell, Jack Goacher, Peter Hayward and a student.

Waterworks Valley, late 1940s. During the Second World War a large part of Norton Farm was used by the army as a shelling range and several of the plantations in the Waterworks Valley were blown to pieces. They were originally planted by Mr Somerville, one-time owner of Denton Hill Farm. Here the timber and stumps are being cleared out after the war.

The drawing room, Stud Farm, c. 1934. Stud Farm was built in the early years of this century by Captain Masters. By 1934 Mr and Mrs F. Collinson lived here. For some years after, the stables were used jointly by Mr Collinson and F.D. Pirie to keep their racehorses.

Stud Farm hostel, late 1940s. Stud Farm was used during and after the Second World War by the War Agricultural Department as a hostel for ex-servicemen and trainee farm students. Above, left to right: Peter Hayward and others nicknamed 'Blakey', 'Switch' and 'Flighty'. The fifth man is Bill Laws, Switch's brother. Below, left to right: matron, looking out of the window, Peter Hayward, Bill Laws, Switch and Blakey.

Section Five

DOWN THE ROAD
TOWARDS THE SEA

Telephone Hill, c. 1948. The hill was so named because
in the 1930s it had a signpost pointing towards the village,
which stated: 'You may telephone from here. ½ mile.' Jim
Westwood of New Cottages is on his daily walk to the
Buckle Inn . . . and so we make our way down the road
towards the sea.

Nos. 11–27 Bishopstone Road, *c*. 1958. Most of the bungalows were built before the Second World War by Alfred Hall, and cost £700. The 1936 sales particulars stated: general rate for Seaford: 9*s* 1*d* in the pound; water rate: 1*s* 7*d* in the pound; electricity: 8*d* per unit for lighting and ½*d* per unit for power and heating.

Nos. 4–11 Bishopstone Road, *c*. 1958. As usual, villagers have propped their bicycles against Mrs W. Hunt's hedge at 4 Bishopstone Road and gone to catch their buses and trains. If one travelled to London by train in 1936 the season ticket rates were: three months: £11 4*s* 6*d*; one month: £5 0*s* 6*d*; weekend return: 10*s*; cheap day 7*s* 6*d*.

Lionel Willett's Sussex cattle, Newlands, *c.* 1947. On the other side of the wall is the main road, and the crossroads are just to the right. Further in the background is the chalk pit, where many an altercation broke out with the gypsies who pitched camp there.

From Marine Drive towards Hawth Hill. In 1962 work started on cutting out the Buckle bypass. In the centre is the thatched office formerly used by the Guildhall Development Company for promoting the estate (see page 16).

Buckle bypass, 1962. All the chalk from the top of Hawth Hill was moved to fill in Valley Dip. The bypass was first thought about in the early 1930s, but it was another thirty years before it was actually constructed.

Earth-moving tractors, summer 1962. The tractors are on top of Hawth Hill, during construction of the bypass. In the distance are the Surrey Convalescent Home and Tudor Close.

The Buckle Inn, *c.* 1912. For those who lived in Bishopstone this was the nearest place to go for a drink. Originally a row of farm cottages, it served the communities of Bishopstone, Tidemills and the Coastguards. For many years the Venus family were landlords and, despite being nearly in the sea, they had a wonderful garden beside the Buckle arch, surrounded by tamarisk hedges, and took many a prize at the produce shows.

Outside the Buckle, 1947. Left to right: Doris and Len Hambling and their cousins Alan and Toni Laughlin. 'Cheers and Good Health!' as we leave the last building in Bishopstone.

Buckle beach, 1947. During the war years, the beach was out of bounds due to mines, barbed wire, etc. It was therefore a treat to go down to the beach once they had been cleared. Left to right: Lord and Lady Asquith, Betty McConnel and a friend are enjoying the summer of 1947 (see page 44).

Buckle beach, late 1940s. Left to right: Jack Saunders, Percy Cox, Bob Moore, 'Smokie' Everest and Dyllis Brook.

TIDEMILLS TO CUCKMERE HAVEN

Steam trawler Gamecock *aground, 1908. In a September gale the crew of the Hull trawler found that they were short of fuel and unable to make enough headway to keep off the beach opposite Tidemills village. They temporarily abandoned the vessel with its catch still aboard and were brought ashore one by one in the canvas 'breeches' on a line fired from shore by rocket. The fish made fine ammunition for that year's battle between the village boys and their townie enemies, the Brooklyn Road gang. Patched up, the* Gamecock *returned to Hull for repairs; three months later she set off for the North Sea, and was never seen again.*

The millhouse, *c.* 1883. From his country seat, Bishopstone Place, the Duke of Newcastle overlooked the course of the old east-flowing river Ouse. He conceived the idea of building a mill across the still-tidal creek, for which he received parliamentary approval in 1761. Barges would be on hand to transport the flour and grain by river and sea. There were originally five pairs of grinding stones, but, when the Catt family took over thirty years later, they increased the capacity to sixteen pairs. Sixty men and their families lived in Tidemills village in its heyday.

The granary and creek, 1901. By judicious control of the sluice gates and millponds in conjunction with the tides of the creek, miller William Catt achieved the maximum number of hours of work. During the Napoleonic wars he supplied flour to most of Sussex, including many of the troops drafted into hastily built camps in the coastal areas, in readiness for invasion. In 1795 a sloop, the *Lucy*, was stolen from here with her cargo of flour by mutinying soldiers in protest at poor living conditions.

Workers' cottages, 1930s. The advent of rail transport and steam-driven mills put an end to the tidemills' usefulness. The creek was closed to barge traffic and the cottages used by employees of the new owners, Newhaven Harbour Company. Materials from ships wrecked nearby continued to be put to good use; stout timbers made strong fences.

The Larkin boys, c. 1917. Brothers Fred (left) and Bill lived at Tidemills and attended Bishopstone village school (see pages 24 and 28). Among other Tidemills families were the Tubbs, the Geerings and the Wilmshursts. In the years before the Second World War, the community was enlarged by people living in former railway coaches, established on the beach; Mr David Dale and his staff ran a racehorse training stables at the old millhouse.

Sea defences near the Buckle Inn, *c*. 1948. From the earliest attempt to defend this part of the bay with a sea wall, almost a century ago, various techniques have been used. Little maintenance could be carried out during the years of the Second World War, and severe storms in October and December 1945 left several major breaches, including two over 200 feet long. Parts of the town suffered the worst flooding for seventy years.

Buckle to Claremont Road, *c.* 1950. The kiosk on the left had seen service as a Second World War gun turret and an ice-cream sales point. Major repairs to the seawall around groyne 23 were the result of consultation with engineers Sir William Halcrow and Partners. During these repairs the logo of the Demolition and Construction Co. Ltd was displayed on the kiosk. This company undertook the installation of sheet piling faced with reinforced concrete panels and wooden shuttering, with a bull-nose coping. In front of the telegraph pole on the right is one of the boilers which supplied steam for the pile-driver.

West Parade opposite Connaught Road, 1930s. In the middle distance are the southernmost Sea Cottages, the old coastguards' houses. Buckle Rise now occupied the site. Behind the strolling holiday-makers stands a neat row of wooden changing huts, successors to the bathing machines and bell tents of earlier, more modest days.

West Parade, 17 September 1935. Local photographer John Ball recorded a chaotic scene after a night of storms. Within five years this part of the seafront was differently devastated when the houses in the middle distance, including Weather Point and Palazzuola (which had its own small chapel), were taken over by the 130 men of 343 Heavy Battery with two 6-inch naval guns and searchlights. People continued living in nearby Claremont Road and were told in advance when practice shoots would take place. By opening all doors and windows, residents reduced the risk of blast damage.

Seafront shelter opposite Dane Road, 1930s. Opened in about 1910, this was the last word in design to afford promenaders a respite from stiff sea-breezes without loss of marine views. The shelter was nevertheless sited in a vulnerable spot. It was severely damaged by high seas in 1935, when the telephone kiosk was flattened. Final demolition followed another storm in 1940.

Esplanade near West View. The railway station was opened on 1 June 1864 and held promise of making Seaford 'a second Brighton'. Schemes were started which might have resulted in a congestion of hotels, boarding houses, shops, restaurants and amusement palaces, as sported by its jauntier neighbour, but disputes between developers together with lack of funds dictated otherwise. The healthy properties of Seaford's air and its sea-bathing facilities were among the attractions from Victorian times (above) to the 1930s (below), with an occasional regatta, concert, fireworks display or 'conversazione' to relieve the peace and quiet.

Looking north-west from the Martello Tower. Published by Alex Rankin, stationer of Newhaven and Seaford, this postcard shows very clearly the old course of the river Ouse, in the low-lying fields between the seafront and Steyne Road. Tons of chalk were used to build raised roads such as the Causeway, Ringmer Road and St John's Road. These gave safe passage across land which was liable to flood. It remained so until the 1980s, when drainage work was done prior to the development of The Covers and The Boundary.

Martello Tower number 74, *c.* 1910. The tower was the last of the south-east chain to be built and was not completed until after the Battle of Trafalgar in 1805. It never played a part in the threatened French invasion. After some desultory use as a coastguard station and signal post, it was allowed to fall into disrepair until taken over in 1910 by Mr Tom Funnell. His schemes included a tea room, a museum, sea-water baths and a roller-skating circuit in the lower-level dry moat around the tower. In 1979 it was restored by the owner, Lewes District Council, and since then it has housed Seaford Museum of Local History.

The stone groyne, Splash Point, 1930s. This long groyne was vitally important in preventing excessive shingle loss from Seaford's beaches. Near this spot, in 1850, army engineers set off explosive charges in the cliff face, bringing down some 380,000 tons of chalk intended to form a permanent natural groyne to deflect unwelcome sea-currents. The 400-feet high, 300-feet long bank fell as planned but was soon washed away by the very waves it was meant to control. The crowd is gathered at the head of the iron ladder leading down to the far beach.

Sea-defence work, Splash Point, 1950. A sudden drop of 15 feet in beach levels was noticed, and urgent repair work put in hand. The 35-ton crane with hammer (pile-driver) was too heavy to be worked from above the site, so this gantry was built. The brick wall just visible on the clifftop is the original boundary of Splash Point Hotel; the wall still stands but the hotel was demolished because of cliff erosion.

Access to the beach from Seaford Head. Tales abound of ill-advised young men attempting to climb down to the beach from the clifftop. Sometimes this was done for devilment but occasionally for other reasons, as sadly recorded in the parish church register for 1796: 'June 6. Buried John Cosstick accidentally killed by falling down the cliff, by endeavouring to take the Mew's (gull's) eggs.' The message on the postcard of Puck Church gap (left) is 'Feeling much refreshed by Seaford air.' It was written in 1927: the gap is not now accessible. However, Hope Gap (below) can still be reached via South Hill Barn and Hope Bottom. Steps were renewed in 1931 and 1950.

A family picnic, *c*. 1910. The original of this photograph was a faded sepia, with a message written in French. It conveys the Edwardian era's attitude to a day by the sea: there are no concessions to the informal setting, except perhaps the girls being bareheaded. We wonder if they are aware of the risks of being stranded between the foot of the cliff and the incoming tide?

Cuckmere Haven from Short Cliff. In Napoleonic times a barracks comprising two officers' buildings, four soldiers' buildings, two magazines and barrack-master's building stood on the lower slopes of Haven Brow, the first of the Seven Sisters cliffs. Some of the foundations can still be found. A caravan and camping site existed in the area in the 1950s and 1960s, but the land now forms part of the 700-acre Seven Sisters Country Park. Over 300 acres of meadow, cliff and foreshore on the town side of the Haven have become Seaford Head Nature Reserve, habitat of rare plants and birds. The shore hereabouts is famous for the marine wildlife to be found in its rockpools.

Coastguards' cottages, summer 1949. They were essential to guard the Haven, regarded by smugglers as a fine landing place. From here contraband could be ferried up the river to Alfriston, or carried by man or pony along the clifftop to Seaford. Seizures reported by customs men – sometimes after bloody (even fatal) clashes – included 'five horses and twelve nine-gallon casks of foreign spirits taken' – 'forty-two tubs of spirits of Geneva which the smugglers could well spare from their cargo of 340' – 'sixty casks of spirits'. The smugglers called the customs men 'Justice Johns'.

Refreshment hut, *c*. 1910. The hut, which must have been a boon to walkers and campers alike, can also be seen in the background of the next photograph. Though a delightful spot to sit with a cooling drink on a fine summer's day, its proximity to a stormy sea would have made it uncomfortable in winter.

Camping at Cuckmere, 1912. Published by A. Beal of The Library, High Street, Seaford, this postcard view was sent by someone staying at Bainbridge House. This was a Swiss-chalet-style rest home for shop girls off Steyne Road, endowed by philanthropist Emerson Bainbridge in 1900. In the distance are the refreshment hut and coastguards' cottages, seen on earlier pages, and the old boat-house which survived till sea defence works in 1949.

Sunset, 1930s. Some devotees of Sir Arthur Conan Doyle's Sherlock Holmes tales say that Cuckmere Haven was the inspiration for Fulworth Cove in *The Adventure of the Lion's Mane*, featuring the great detective in retirement. The opening paragraphs of the story could certainly be a description of the Haven. Those who are familiar with this stretch of coast may find their knowledge leads to a speedy solution of the mystery.

The Cuckmere, 1920s. The river's picturesque meanders were awkward to navigate and did nothing to relieve the problem of silting up of the river mouth. In 1846, by manual labour only, gangs of men cut the straight canal from the sea to Exceat Bridge. The postcard view of the path from Friston Forest (left) was sent on 4 September 1922 by a guest at Denmark House, Steyne Road, Seaford, to office colleagues in London's Aldwych, commenting on the swimming and walking he was enjoying. The lower picture is from a study by prize-winning local photographers Tester Brothers.

The Golden Galleon restaurant, 1960s. When the restaurant was built earlier this century, it was claimed that old ships' timbers were among the materials used, hence the name. Its delightful situation, next to the former shepherd's cottage and looking across the Cuckmere valley towards the sea, has ensured its continuing popularity, in spite of inevitable changes of ownership, and a disastrous fire in 1969.

Looking upstream from Exceat Bridge, 1930s. Canoes and other small craft could be hired from the refreshment cabin on the left, known as the Boat-house. The row up to Drusilla's tea gardens at Alfriston was a pleasant one and passed the white horse landmark cut in the chalk on Hindover Hill. Campers pitched their tents along the bank where, a century before, smugglers such as Stanton Collins and his gang drove their ponies to the village, loaded with tobacco, spirits and other contraband.

Aerial view, 1931. The valley presented a very different aspect in 1925 when the Cuckmere burst its banks and flooded the meadows up to Alfriston, where the main road was awash. Further disasters were avoided by raising banks and paths to designs by Dutch engineers.

Gently flows the Cuckmere. The quiet setting of the valley still draws walkers, campers, photographers, ornithologists and other lovers of the countryside. The loss of many willow trees along the banks is one of the greatest changes to this lovely part of Sussex.

STREETS AND
BUILDINGS

The Green Tea Rooms, 1928. In the 1920s the tea rooms at 19 Pelham Road were run by the
Misses Upton and Robson and in the next decade by the Misses Loader and Jacobs who later
renamed it the Wander-In. After the Second World War it was called the Chantecler by new
proprietor Miss Doris Bedford. The buildings in this part of Pelham Road were intended to form a
parade of shops but did not prosper. Most were converted into private homes or boarding-houses,
although the unusually large front windows remained for years.

Pelham Place, *c.* 1905. The London to Newhaven railway line was extended to Seaford in 1864, and 'a second Brighton' began to rise in terraces of purpose-built boarding houses. Pelham Place was built in 1867–8, one of only a few such terraces ever completed. In one of the houses on the far left, some ninety years ago, lived young Clementine Hozier (later Lady Churchill). When a bomb fell here during the Second World War, her former home was one of those destroyed.

Looking towards the Steyne and South Street, *c.* 1900. On old maps the Steyne (now Steyne Road) was shown as Le Quayside and fronted the harbour whose existence entitled Seaford to membership of the ancient Cinque Ports system. Though all but the most distant of the buildings here remain, development of the open land in the foreground (formerly that of the harbour) prevents this view being seen today.

The Pavement, Church Street, 1903. Even today not much has changed: the trees have gone; the shops bear different trade names and advertisements; and the pointed arch on the right (offering 'open and closed rubber-tyred carriages' for hire, and livery stables) no longer marks the entrance to Church Mews. Horses were still stabled here in the 1930s, though part of the old premises, then as now, were used as a furniture store. This view is part of a novelty 'Panoramicard' 11½ inches long and 3½ inches deep, still requiring only a ha'penny postage 'if no communication be written beyond sender's name'.

The old Town Hall before 1922. It was on these steps, if legend is to be believed, that the clerk of Seaford corporation once stood holding a book in which the lord of the manor was able to record his vote while still on horseback. The tiny Elizabethan building originally served as courtroom, prison and civic centre, and has since had a variety of uses. In spite of major changes, including the removal of the steps and porch in the 1920s and total refurbishment after fire gutted it in 1989, it has survived for over 430 years.

Station entrance and Clinton Place, 1930s. Clinton Place was originally called Terminus Road, for it led westwards only to the railway station. A gate (far left) marked the entrance to the station forecourt and the goods yard beyond. The three-storey house in the centre still stands on the corner of Claremont Road and Blatchington Road (opening behind the cyclist). The imposing corner store with sunblinds was then Hoadley's draper's, and, far right, was ironmonger George Woolgar's shop, with steps up to the corner door.

Claremont Road from Station Approach. Until 1876 the only direct route from Seaford to the Buckle and on to Newhaven was the coast road. As erosion caused the beach to encroach, the sea often came perilously close to the road at high tides. After any flooding, rowing boats replaced carts and carriages. Far left are the distant buildings of the station goods yard, now re-developed as St Crispian's estate. The new road's name was probably an association with the Pelham family's country seat, Claremont, at Esher, Surrey.

Seaside convalescent home. The home originated in 1860 in Augusta House, Lower High Street (see page 104), where some wealthy young men set up a 'halfway house' for people discharged from hospital but not yet fit to resume work. It is thought to have been the first establishment of its kind in this country. Such was the demand for places that, within a decade, it became necessary to move to purpose-built premises (above) on a site facing the sea, between Crooked Lane and Bramber Road. These buildings continued to serve as a recuperative/holiday centre for visitors such as those pictured below in the 1930s. The home was demolished in the 1960s; the site was then redeveloped as the Bramber Close/Steyne Close estate. Part of this land had once been 'Hangman's Acre', granted to the local executioner in recognition of his gruesome duties.

Demolition of Sutton Mill, 1904. The mill was built in 1769 for Mr Thomas Washer (see page 104). Only four years later little James Stevens stood too near to the building and 'was killed by a sweep of Mr Washer's windmill', as recorded in the parish register. The post mill continued to produce flour until 1900, when the sails were removed. Final demolition took place four years later. The millhouse still survives, on the eastern corner of Sutton Road, opposite Southdown Road.

Towards Blachington from Sutton Drove, 1920s. In the foreground on the left are Park Cottages, a terrace of four houses at right angles to Sutton Drove. The Clymax and The Limit had yet to be built on the land bounded by the flint wall. Down the hill on the right are some of the earlier houses in Vale Road and, behind, the remains of North Camp. This was a vast hutted community created during the First World War for thousands of British and Empire troops in training and en route for the trenches of France and Belgium.

Surrey convalescent home, East Blatchington, *c.* 1907. Seaford's second major convalescent establishment stood on land off Claremont Road, north of the railway line. The site is now occupied by Surrey Road, Bishops Close and neighbouring roads. On Christmas Eve 1888, while the home was being built, the *Mary Davis* was wrecked on the beach less than a mile away. All her crew survived and part of the cargo of Portland stone was bought by the home's builders for £20 and incorporated into the stairs and landings. Patients often posed for photographs with Joey the donkey and his cart (see right), or with Cocky the cockatoo.

Blatchington Street, looking north, *c.* 1905. The spire of St Peter the Apostle church (left) was struck by lightning on 30 December 1879 and a brass plate on the west wall gives thanks for the building being spared. The chimneys showing above the trees belong to the Old Rectory. The building on the extreme right (with the mouth of Homefield Road immediately beyond) was formerly the Star Inn. It is said that the village stocks stood on the opposite corner (lower left) until about 1840.

Stafford Road from East Albany Road, early 1930s. The Ordnance Survey map of the urban district of Seaford, dated 1928, shows a road with few buildings connecting the northern end of Broad Street with East Albany Road. Eventually more than one hundred houses and bungalows appeared; here Ferndown (later 97 Stafford Road) has yet to be built. The back gardens of these properties overlooked Sutton Drove, a drop of some feet down the hillside.

The silver band, Crouchfield. Before Crouchfield became a hotel, it was the home of the Danby family. The last resident was Miss Gertrude E. Danby BEM, JP, a leading citizen and good friend of the town. The bank was probably about to play for some civic or charitable event being held there at her invitation. The old local word 'crouch' is thought to mean 'cross' (where paths intersect); near here was an ancient parcel of land known as Crouch Field. The hotel was demolished in 1966 and the Constitutional Club now occupies the site.

Section Eight

EVENTS AND PEOPLE

Mrs Sarah Kimber Simmons, c. 1870. Several generations
of the Simmons family had already traded as bootmakers
when this photograph was taken outside their premises in
Church Street (where the police station now stands). As time
went by, the shop became more of a tobacconist's and
sweetshop; specialities included home-made humbugs. One of
Mrs Simmons's customers was 'Catty' West, an old sailor
who had been at the Battle of Trafalgar in 1805.

Newhaven/Seaford rail link, 1864. The passenger service from London to Newhaven had been in operation since late in 1847 and plans for an extension to Seaford were put forward three times, each time unsuccessfully. In 1862 an omnibus connection with many Newhaven trains was established. At last the approaches of an action committee of leading citizens to the London Brighton and South Coast Railway were favourably received and work began on the 2¼-mile track. Opening day, 1 June 1864, was marked with free travel, bunting decorating Tidemills village, a procession and a self-congratulatory dinner.

Old folks' celebratory meal, Church Street School hall, *c.* 1900. Seaford's senior citizens were not overlooked when the rest of the town had something to celebrate. The peace day programme for Saturday 19 July 1919 included a midday 'dinner for adults over 65 in the Simmons Institute'. We believe an earlier event is shown here, perhaps part of the festivities for King Edward VII's coronation in 1902. Unfortunately the only writing on the reverse is a shopping list!

Mr Henry Simmons, *c.* 1895. Mr Simmons was bailiff of Seaford for four terms and, in 1858, led a deputation from the corporation (dressed in full court finery of frock-coats, frilled shirts, knee-breeches, silk stockings and buckled shoes) to present a loyal address to Queen Victoria on the betrothal of her eldest daughter. He gave generously to help the poor and elderly and built the Simmons Institute in Crouch Lane for community use. Simmons is a popular Seaford name, derived from earlier spellings Seaman and Seman; it first appears in official records dated 1296.

THOMAS CROOK.
FOUNDER of the GAS WORKS.

Mr Thomas Crook, founder of the gasworks. Mr Crook formed the Seaford Gas Company in 1860 with three retorts at works in Blatchington Road. He had the intention of laying pipes throughout the town, not entirely enthusiastically received by the townspeople. He leased the West Gun Field (the corner of Dane Road and the Esplanade) from the corporation and built his family home Telsemaure there: it was the first Seaford house to be lit by gas. The letters spelling 'Telsemaure' were the initials of members of his family (Thomas, Elizabeth, Lewis, and so on).

Proclamation of the accession of King Edward VII, 1901. Seaford Urban District Council came into being in December 1894 and, three years later, moved its offices from the old Town Hall (page 85) to 3 Clinton Place, where this ceremony took place. The wrought-iron balcony is decorated with representations of the royal arms and Seaford's ancient seals. The hollow square of spectators is lined by militiamen. Nearby, lads wearing pillbox headgear are probably cadets from Seaford College.

Albert Fowler, Sutton Road, 1908. A number of tradesmen managed without shop premises and conducted their business from a horse and cart or even coster-barrow. They knocked at doors or announced their arrival in the street with some distinctive call. The knife-grinder and the mender of cane-seated chairs were two without premises and worked at the roadside. Roast chestnuts, balloons and hokey-pokey (ice-cream) were dispensed from smaller barrows.

Coronation day, 22 June 1911. A grand procession was one of the events organized to celebrate the crowning of King George V and Queen Mary. The boy scout band (above) forms up beneath a triumphal arch in Sutton Park Road near the junction with Upper Broad Street: the spire of the Congregational church can be seen on the right. The column of marchers and decorated floats stretches back along Terminus Road (Clinton Place), passing under the fire brigade's escape ladders, extended to form an inverted 'V' arch. The wagon carrying Church Street school's May Queen and her attendants (below) was in the procession. The cart was loaned by Mr E.A. Simmonds, coal merchant, who is on the far right of the picture.

Surrey convalescent home, 1909. Mr Bryce, sixth man from the right in the background, carrying a flag of the royal standard, wrote on the reverse of this photograph: 'Monday July 12th 1909. Patients waiting to receive HRH Duke of Teck who didn't turn up. Admiral FitzGeorge apologised for his absence (the Duke's). A grand day. Several nobles and knights and a good tuck-in.' In the Second World War the home was requisitioned as quarters for a unit of the Women's Royal Naval Service. The site was sold for redevelopment in 1966 and is now occupied by the houses and bungalows of Friston Close, Jevington Drive and the original Surrey Road.

Driver Reg Fears. Young Mr Fears drove for French's garage, established in 1912 in Steyne Road. Early garages not only sold motor cars and parts, especially tyres (most vehicles had a spare wheel mounted outside on the running-board or the boot), but also offered other services. Garages routinely hired cars and ran taxis and sometimes also recharged cumbersome acid-filled glass batteries.

Peace day procession, 1919. On Saturday 19 July the nation held celebrations for the end of the First World War. Seaford's organizing committee, chaired by Mr Tom Godfrey, produced a programme which began with this procession. It went from the parish church to the Alfriston Road cemetery for a short service and the placing of flowers on the graves of the fallen. Two years later the British Legion was founded for ex-servicemen, and Seaford's Comrades of the Great War re-formed as one of the earliest branches.

The war memorial, 1921. This Cornish granite memorial was dedicated on 3 August 1921 at its site on the eastern corner of Dane Road and Green Lane. After the Second World War, with many more names to add, the damage suffered by exposure to sea-winds was repaired and the memorial re-designed and re-sited at the junction of Sutton Park Road and Avondale Road. It now bears a total of 219 names from the Boer War and the First and Second World Wars and includes twenty civilians killed in air raids.

Decorated donkey cart, *c*. 1910. A number of early photographs exist showing Seaford people in strange costumes, either to celebrate occasions such as peace day 1919, royal jubilees and coronations, or to raise funds for worthy causes such as the hospital, by comic cricket matches and carnivals. This group includes Bert Banks, Bert and Ernie Pettitt and possibly Bill Green.

Hindover hill, 1921. The early motorcycles gathered above Hindover for hill-climbing trials have several interesting obsolete features, including the central sidecar's wheel, fitted with a metal disc mudguard. Before sidecars existed motorcycles towed additional passengers in wicker carts known as Montgomery trailers. Humber, a name better known in car manufacture, were early motorcycle builders.

Bells of the parish church, 1923. In 1811 churchwardens John Gatland and William Nicholas bought a new peal of bells from Mears of Whitechapel. In 1923 re-casting, new frames and a new belfry floor cost £793. The bells were delivered (by London Brighton and South Coast Railway) in time to be rung on Christmas morning. Included in this group are the Revd E.H. Phillips MA (vicar), Mr Albert Simmons (sexton, in braces), Mr Thomas Fisher (people's warden), Mrs Fisher, Mr James, and Mr Oliver Ford representing the railway.

The laying of the foundation stone of Clinton Hall, June 1924. The first hall of this name, built on the corner of Upper Broad Street and Clinton Lane in 1890, burned down twenty-eight years later. It had been used by the Congregational church (see page 95) for a Sunday school, classroom and meeting-hall. Local builders Godfrey Brothers erected the new hall for about £3,000, most of it raised by the Revd G.W. Berry and his committee.

Blatchington Pond, *c.* 1922. The rising footpath still links Sutton Drove (running across the top of the picture) to Avondale Road. The distant fields are now built over and have become Sherwood Road and Vale Road. In over seventy years the trees have matured so that it is no longer possible to stand here and see across. On the extreme right is the boundary of properties in Stafford Road (see page 90).

Ussuri aground, June 1936. Returning from Algiers to Rotterdam with a ballast cargo of water, the Russian vessel went off course in fog and ran up the beach opposite the Salts recreation ground; her bow touched the rim of the seawall. Offers of help from Newhaven tugs were refused and the *Ussuri's* female wireless operator summoned a sister ship, the *Perekof*, to cross the Channel to tow the *Ussuri* off. Several of the ship's complement of twenty cats seized the opportunity to jump ashore and run off.

Salts recreation ground, 1954. Severe flooding of the low-lying ground behind the seawall gave an idea of how the area must have looked in medieval times when the river Ouse flowed towards its mouth near the foot of Seaford Head. The floodwater was already receding when the photographs were taken: it had been 4 feet 6 inches deep, almost covering the old figurehead displayed in front of the café. She had earlier stood on the Esplanade, and is now at the Martello Tower in the care of Seaford Museum. The recreation ground's name is a reminder of the days when salt could be found in evaporated sea-water pools, left when the tide turned. This precious commodity was used not only for flavouring but as an essential food preservative.

Firefighters on parade, Church Street, early 1940s. The Auxiliary Fire Service was set up as part of the Air Raid Precautions (ARP) system (civil defence) when war seemed imminent at the end of the 1930s. The name was later changed to the National Fire Service (NFS). The fire station was in Dane Road near the war memorial when the latter was sited there. Behind the firemen, in this morale-boosting parade of uniformed civilians, is a large contingent of wardens and other ARP personnel. In the top left-hand corner is the bombsite which also appears on the facing page.

Bomb damage, West Street 1941. On 1 April 1941, just after 7.30 in the evening, a lone enemy raider dropped a stick of high explosive bombs on the town centre. One, which fell near the south-east corner of Pelham Road and West Street, at the rear of the Bay Hotel (from which this photograph was taken), virtually wiped out the buildings in Chatham Place and West Street. In the left foreground is the hotel garage with Mareesh House behind and part of Elm Villas beyond. The buildings partially obscuring the church on the left also suffered a direct hit, with a fatality at Kennard's dairy, 41 Church Street.

First aid post personnel, Second World War. Ambulance drivers, nurses and other first aid workers include Mrs Libeau, Miss Randall, Miss Winifred Synge (driver), Mr Colin Cameron, Mr Les Lambert, Mr George Laughlin, Mr Frank Nail (in leader's white helmet), Mr Jack Shinn and Mr Bill Urry. Seaford had 1,053 'alerts' (when the warning sirens sounded) and more than forty 'incidents' (bombs dropped or other hostile activity such as machine-gun attacks).

Church Street, 1946. Damaged buildings and the flattened bombsite on the south corner of West Street, behind the cyclist, are reminders of the war recently over. In 1969 the police station was moved from Chichester Road to purpose-built premises on this site, and, ten years later, the post office was erected on the fenced-off corner behind the young pedestrians, Miss Keeble and Miss Price-Jones.

Parish church bell-ringers, 1948. In the bell-ringing chamber are Mr Sexton (left) and Mr Simmons; the board behind them gives names of the ringers of a historic peal in 1892. From parochial records we know there to have been bells in the church since the early eighteenth century, if not earlier. Various commemorative tablets around the building tell of the efforts made over the years to maintain them (see page 99).

Talland, Lower High Street, 1964. Built in 1714 for Mr Washer of Sutton Mill (page 88) and, when known as Augusta House, occupied in 1860 by the Seaside convalescent home (page 87), this once-elegant house fell into disrepair after post-war use as a guest-house. The site had been considered – and rejected – for both a cinema and new British Legion headquarters, after their premises in Pelham Road were bombed. Shops and offices were eventually erected on the site (eradicating yet another ancient flint wall in the process) but the old house lives on in the name Talland Parade.

Section Nine

YOUTH

Coronation procession, 1911. Many young people paraded

through the streets of Seaford on 22 June 1911 to celebrate

the coronation of King George V and Queen Mary. In the

foreground are convalescent home nurses and warrior

maidens waiting in Claremont Road; on the embankment

behind them are the railway station buildings and the road

to the goods yard. The festive day ended spectacularly with

the parish church outlined in gaslight.

Sunday school treat, *c.* 1910. The traction engine, owned by French's garage (see page 96), was much in demand in the summer months for driving the threshing machines or drawing wagonloads of pupils to their favourite outing venues. For rural children, the seaside might be a sufficient change of scene: somewhere like Litlington tea gardens was more often chosen for classes from Seaford.

Church Street infants, *c.* 1912. Mr J.P. FitzGerald built a school in Steyne Road in 1858 for the town children. A separate girls' establishment opened in Church Street twenty-one years later. Miss Amy Chambers's infants' department opened alongside it in 1889. She kept a diary of school events recording both good and bad times. Days off for coronations, royal weddings or the relief of Ladysmith were entered as well as gifts of ice-cream, oranges and 'a splendid Guy' for 5 November. Sad occasions included the death of a teacher in the influenza epidemic of 1918/19, and the honouring of the thirty-four young men, former pupils, lost in the First World War.

Infants' department, Empire Day, 1912. Miss Chambers maintained the traditions of May Day and Empire Day by devising an annual pageant or other ceremony. In 1912 the May Day prizes were presented by Lady Bromley. Her eldest son Cuthbert was, only three years later, posthumously awarded the Victoria Cross for valour at Gallipoli. Empire Day was instituted after the South African war, and has been celebrated as Commonwealth Day since 1959.

Seaford Ladies' College, 1933. This postcard view of the front hall was sent to a former pupil with a birthday message from two of the principals, Miss A. Paine and Miss M. Witherington. The purpose-built premises in Eastbourne Road still stand and are still a school, although the college closed in 1953. A three-light stained glass window in the north wall of the parish church commemorates the fifty-three years during which generations of young ladies worshipped there.

1st Blatchington Girl Guides (above) proudly display their company banner, made by the Rangers (senior Guides). Some of the latter went on to become founder members of Seaford Trefoil Guild for those who formerly belonged to the movement. Motifs on the banner represent (left to right) the Guide trefoil; mythical Sussex birds and county symbol, the martlets; a Cinque Ports ship; a ten-pointed star (one point for each of the Guide laws); the company motto 'Excelsior'. Ranger Captain Mrs Martley (left) had over forty years' service to Guiding. At one stage both the 1st Blatchington and 2nd Seaford companies had the use of a room at a local builder's (Morling's, Brooklyn Road) works for meetings. The Salts recreation ground (below) was conveniently near for outdoor activities.

Seaford Boys School cricket team, 1929. School staff and winners of the trophy have been identified as Mr Phillips (headmaster), Mr Cockleton, Mr West and Mr Stevens, George Bartlett, Ted Carr, Arthur Chapman, ? Cook, Dougie Jakens, Maurice Lowles, Harry Marshall, Charlie Rush, Spencer Smith, George Sowter and Ted Warrell. At this time, the boys' department of the town school was in Steyne Road on the corner of Crooked Lane.

Kingsmead School, 1927. This boys' preparatory school had royal visitors in 1935. King George V was resting at Compton Place, Eastbourne, in preparation for the strenuous silver jubilee celebrations to take place in May. He and Queen Mary drove to pay an informal call on their godson Mr Peter Beck who taught at the school. The buildings have long since been adapted for nursing home and residental uses, but the name Kingsmead remains in the names of roads developed on the former playing fields.

Church Street School, 1930s. The children are taking part in a later version of Miss Chambers' May Day celebration (see page 107). One of the boys is Dennis Rowlands (far left). In 1936, members of the girls' school acted in a play *Fireworks in Sussex* (below). Fifty-five years later, shortly before the primary school left Church Street for new premises off Belgrave Road, a reunion of former scholars was held, at which fifteen of the original *Fireworks* cast were photographed together once more. (The lower picture is reproduced here by kind permission of the *Sussex Express & County Herald*.)

Chesterton School, *c*. 1930. Founded in 1910, the school stood in 12 acres of playing fields (above) to the north of Eastbourne Road. By the mid-1950s, when Mr R.L. Hayes was headmaster, some fifty boys boarded there. Swimming, gymnastics, shooting, boxing and (optional) riding and dancing were then among physical activities. A pre-war sports meeting is in progress in the lower photograph.

Evacuees leave Seaford, *c.* 1941. In the early days of the Second World War mothers and children were evacuated from London to the supposed safety of the Seaford district. It was soon realized, however, that coastal areas were also vulnerable to enemy attack. Local children leaving Seaford railway station for Bedford are, top row, left to right: Peggy Bartholomew, Kath Green, Barbara Bernthal, Pat Bartholomew; bottom rows: Edna Green, Rosa Bernthal, Dorothy Bernthal.

Young people's party, 7 January 1946. Only a few months after the end of the Second World War, rationing and shortages were overcome by the mothers and British Legion women's section members who organized this entertainment. Among the children are Sheila Balkham, Thirza Earl, Pam Hayter, John Isted, Hazel Jones, Eileen Jordan, Geoff Killick, Ian Lavender, Ken Parry, Neil Peckham, Phil Satchell and Michael Smith.

Senior boys' football team, 1953. The Senior Modern School (boys and girls) opened in Arundel Road in 1938 and, a quarter of a century later in Queen Elizabeth II's Coronation year, the first eleven football team was photographed at the main door. Standing, left to right: J. Brewer, J. Payne, Mr Alexander (teacher), T. Purcell, P. Tuppen, R. Beard, team mascot, Mr Price (headmaster). Seated: J. Isted, D. Lower, ? Cummins, R. Norman, J. Card, -?-, G. Killick.

Seaford Boys' Club social, *c*. 1953. The girls are from Newhaven and are guests of members, who include David Auwkit, Denis Barnes, Terry Barnes, Tony Batup, George Christmas, Johnny Earl, Wilf Guegan, Kenny Hill, David Haynes, John Isted, Geoff Killick, David Lowles, Terry Purcell, Roger Swift, Francis Waite, Brian Whittington, and members of the Baker and Satchell clans.

Paperboys' outing, *c*. 1953. Mr and Mrs Frank Thomas Winser opened a small newsagent's shop in Brooklyn Road in 1896. They moved premises to East Street and again in 1914, to 45 High Street. Two further generations continued the family business until it was sold in 1988. They built up a considerable team of paperboys who, with a 5 a.m. start, delivered daily newspapers all over the town. In the 1950s an annual day out to Southsea by coach was arranged for them by the Winsers. The last of the family to run the business, Mr Terry Winser, recalls the days when newsagents themselves printed the latest cricket scores in their papers' Stop Press columns.

Section Ten

NAVAL AND
MILITARY

Testimonial, 1901. This beautifully executed document marked

the regard of his fellow citizens for Sergeant Percy Pratt on his

return from service in the South African war. It shows the Seven

Sisters cliffs, the Union flag, its pole garlanded with the floral

emblems of Great Britain, the badge of the Royal Engineers, some

detailed rope knots, and the presentation date of 30 May 1901.

Percy went on to become captain of the Seaford fire brigade in

1910. He lived at Thistlebrae, 7 East Street.

Church parade, 1905. The original of this picture was a faded postcard sent by 'Sydney' to his wife in Forest Hill. On manoeuvres at Seaford, he had been searching unsuccessfully for lodgings so that she also could enjoy the change of scene. 'I have marked myself with a cross' he wrote: he is twenty-sixth from the left.

Marching with the troops, c. 1902. With its open spaces and healthy sea air, Seaford was popular with army units for summertime exercises. On the whole the troops were welcome; they brought trade and visitors to the town and returned hospitality with invitations to parades and dinners. However, some said 'There was never a place so ruined . . . noisy and bibulous warriors stalked the streets as if they had bought Sussex and scared quiet visitors with camp-songs.' Small boys had fun striding beside the marching columns and earned 4d for each cannonball retrieved from the sandbank target after firing practices.

Ready for manoeuvres. Grouped outside the railway station, or leaving it via Blatchington Road for their camp site (below, *c.* 1902), men in uniform drew the crowds. An eyewitness account from the 1890s says: 'While they were here they livened the old place up. They had a very fine band and gave a programme of music every evening. The night before going away they were up to all the mischief you could think of. Next morning someone's cart-wheels were up the flagpole, but they paid for any damage they did. When they arrived the town was gaily decorated in welcome.'

Under canvas, 1904. When units first came to Seaford, they were invited by Mr J.P. FitzGerald to make their headquarters at his home, Corsica Hall, but in later years tented camps were pitched. Mock battles, band concerts and fireworks displays enlivened the town for a few weeks each year.

Recruits in training, 1914. Soon after the First World War broke out an army order directed that the 22nd Division of the Third New Army should be sent to Seaford, but billeted in Lewes till the hutted camps were ready. Among the first units to arrive were the 11th Welch Regiment, who found conditions as muddy and unpleasant as they were to meet when sent into battle. In October the 9th North Staffordshires moved in for training. These ten recruits (with their sergeant) have long-barrelled Lee Enfield rifles, as used in the South African war, and only three regimental cap badges between them.

West Indian visitors, c. 1916. Among Empire troops encamped at Seaford were a number from the British West Indian Regiment (BWIR) who stayed for the winter of 1915/16. This photograph suggests that local members of the Ancient Order of Foresters (Cinque Ports Court 7169) played host to some of these soldiers, so far from home. Seaford men are, standing, left to right: W. Dance, Fred Banks, Jack King, Alf Washer, W. Healy, Stan Green. Seated: Dick Bowley, F.W. Pettitt, -?-. There are nineteen graves in Alfriston Road cemetery whose headstones bear the BWIR badge and details of the men who died here.

North Camp, 2 and 3 lines, 1917. An estimated 25,000 soldiers passed through Seaford during the First World War, either for training or to await transport to the battle fronts. When the last troops left they made a presentation to the stationmaster, Mr J.H. Hollindale, for the exceptional work he and his staff had done. Traffic between the camps and the station had been so heavy that roadways sometimes collapsed. North Camp was built on land between Cradle Hill Road and Blatchington Hill; South Camp faced the sea, between Eastbourne and Chyngton Roads.

Off duty in the camps, 1917. The horse and cart (above) is probably bringing supplies from a local shop. It is standing in Sutton Drove with Blatchington Pond in front (see pages 100 and 122). This postcard once belonged to 2009234 C.W. Lizmore, 'E' Company, 3rd Canadian Engineers. The YMCA (Young Men's Christian Association, founded in 1844) provided camps with canteens and facilities for reading, writing letters, Bible studies and recreation. At The Rally (below), men could play billiards or take refreshments including Horlicks Malted Milk, Oxo, or 'Rally Trifle 2d'. Far left is the post office counter, where cards and letters received the camp's own franking.

SPORT AND ENTERTAINMENT

*Miss Dolly Chandler, c. 1910. Dorothy Florence
Chandler, born 29 January 1887, came to
Seaford from Ifield in 1908 and became a member
of Seaford Ladies' Golf Club, Blatchington. As
well as serving as Honorary Secretary of the Club,
she was involved with a number of organizations
in the town, and was a helper at The Rally
(previous page). She died on 30 July 1958.*

Skating on Blatchington pond. The news that the pond had frozen over must have been greeted with pleasure by young and old. It was a rare opportunity to indulge in skating and sliding, or watching others. A young girl's diary of 1887 records: '30 December. Liz and me came round the Blatchington pond and saw some skating.' After some years in decline, the pond in the 1990s is cherished by conservationists and attracts a variety of wildlife.

Early football on the common, c. 1906. Football in Seaford is said to have been started in 1882 by three young men working at the Elm Brewery, Croft Lane. Four years later Seaford Rovers was formed from local men and pupils from Seaford College, then housed at Corsica Hall. Their first captain was a Mr John Major! In 1888, after a replay, they beat Burgess Hill 3–1 to win the Sussex Junior Cup; they were winners again in 1910. For many years the ball used in the latter game, inscribed with the names of both winning teams' members, was a highly prized souvenir.

The Queer Quakers, *c.* 1910. Each summer from about 1900 until the outbreak of war in 1914 Mr Edward Pritchard and his wife Lily brought their troupe of entertainers to Seaford. They set up their marquee in the Dane Road field where Safeway now stands, donned the Puritan costumes which gave them their name, and brought music, colour and comedy to the town. Left to right: Miss Evelyn Heighton, Miss Lily Pritchard, Miss Margaret Bradshaw. The company also included a Russian singer, contralto Nadia Sokoloff (see first selection, page 113).

First hole, Seaford Head golf club, 1920s. These golfers have played off from the first tee opposite the clubhouse in Chyngton Road, clearing Southdown Road to approach the hole on land now occupied by Sunningdale Close. The houses in the background, Polruan, The Bye, Brecon, Skylarks (formerly Underhill) and The White House, have all survived, with the space between Brecon and Underhill since occupied by Firles and Downsway. The clubhouse (far right) has been redeveloped and members now gather in premises at the southern end of Southdown Road. Parts of the course are 300 feet above sea level.

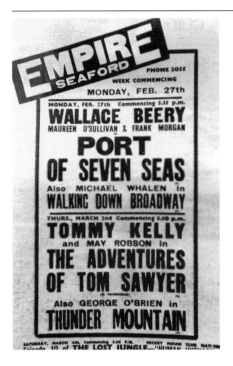

EMPIRE SEAFORD

PHONE 2055

WEEK COMMENCING
MONDAY, FEB. 27th

MONDAY, FEB. 27th Commencing 5.15 p.m.

WALLACE BEERY
MAUREEN O'SULLIVAN & FRANK MORGAN

PORT
OF SEVEN SEAS
Also MICHAEL WHALEN in
WALKING DOWN BROADWAY

THURS., MARCH 2nd Commencing 5.10 p.m.

TOMMY KELLY
and MAY ROBSON in
THE ADVENTURES
OF TOM SAWYER

Also GEORGE O'BRIEN in
THUNDER MOUNTAIN

SATURDAY, MARCH 4th Commencing 5.30 P.M.   MICKEY MOUSE CLUB MATINEE
Episode 10 of THE LOST JUNGLE—"HUMAN

The last picture show, Empire Cinema, 1939. After the cinema closed, on the night of 28 February 1939, fire broke out and the former silent movie-house was gutted. Fireman Fred Mace lost his life fighting the blaze to prevent it spreading to neighbouring homes. An earlier cinema had existed in Brooklyn Road, then the Empire opened in 1913. The Ritz (1936–85) stood on the same corner of Dane Road where the Queer Quakers (page 123) had once set up their marquee.

Anglers at the Buckle, 1960s. From time to time well-intentioned people have suggested that the town could recover its early prosperity by establishing a fishing industry, but the preferred procedure is for anglers to fish independently from the water's edge or from boats in the bay. In season shoals of mackerel can be seen with the naked eye from the beach. It was the custom, in living memory, for the town crier to announce their arrival, prompting a rush to the shore; it has been known for tradesmen's bills to be settled with fish instead of cash.

1 NURSERY RHYMES		...	Ensemble
2 *TAP DUET	...	...	J. Berry G. Tubb
3 BABY PAS de SEUL	...	...	H. Templeton
4 CHARACTER (Caller Herrin)		...	M. Bean
5 MUSICAL COMEDY (Bronze Medal)			W. Beal
6 NATIONAL (French)		...	R. Easton
7 *TAP SOLO	...	...	J. Berry
8 WONDERFUL COPENHAGEN, Danish			V. Gravett
	Swedish		J. Cornwall
	Swedish Shoemaker		Ensemble
	Norwegian		C. Miller
9 *TAP SOLO	...	...	G. Tubb
10 PAS de SEUL	...	...	V. Gravett
11 *TAP SOLO	...	...	J. Cornwall
12 *NATIONAL BATON / PREMARY (babies)			H. Adams / Ensemble
13 *TAP ROUTINE	...	...	Ensemble
14 NATIONAL (Lilt)	...	...	G. Irvine
15 MUSICAL COMEDY	...	...	V. Gravett
16 TAP (Gold Medal)	...	...	R. Easton
17 *BALLET	...	...	Ensemble

INTERVAL

1 WATER LILY	...	...	Ensemble
2 *PAS de SEUL	...	...	M. Bean
3 We must have safety etc.,		...	Ensemble
4 TAP SOLO (Gold Medal)		...	J. Wyatt
5 TYROLEAN Swiss Solo			W. Beal
6 TAP DUET	...	...	M. Bean, V. Gowley
7 SPRING Greek	...	...	Ensemble
8 LOVELY LADY	G. Irvine, J. Berry, G. Tubbs, B. Cornwall
9 NATIONAL (Russian)		...	M. Bean
10 *TAP SOLO	...	...	W. Beal
11 THERE WAS A LITTLE MAN		...	G. Veal
12 NATIONAL (Flemish)		...	J. Berry
13 *MUSICAL COMEDY		...	J. Cornwall
14 GYPSY Fortune Teller		...	C. Goody
15 ...Some crew who			Ensemble
16 PAS de SEUL		...	W. Beal
17 MUSICAL COMEDY	...	...	Ensemble
18 NATIONAL (German Scharm)		...	C. Flegg
19 FINALE		...	The Academy

GOD SAVE THE QUEEN

Seaford's dancing children. Performing tap, national and musical comedy in the 1954 programme of Madame Florence Neal's dancing academy (above) is one J. Cornwall. Under the headline 'Dramatic Society's find in 15-year-old girl' the same young lady, now correctly spelled as Judy Cornwell, received the first of many enthusiastic reviews that have since come her way for stage and television performances. She was appearing at the Queen's Hall, Broad Street. Further performances took place at Eastbourne and Bexhill. The Queen's Hall was also the venue for Seaford Children's Theatre's 1953 pantomime *Robinson Crusoe* (below). The cast included Margaret Banks, Geoff, Jack and Wendy Beal, Pauline Bell, Trixie Jane Bennett, Julie Berry, Leslie Bryant, Jean Everett, Sheila Fears, Caroline Flegg, Pam Forshaw, Glenna and Janine Gasson, Elizabeth and Ken Green, Christine and Julian Hurst, Michael Logan, Georgina and Gill Martin, Clara Morrison, Judy Pelling, Leslie Stoner, Graham Tubb, Brian and Margaret Webb.

Acknowledgements

We should especially like to thank the following for their advice, expertise and reminiscences:

Mr D. Baker • Miss F. Blaber • Miss E. Chandler • Mr and Mrs J.F. Collinson
Mrs S. Dench • Mr and Mrs L. Everest • Mr Frank Haynes
Mr and Mrs P. Hayward • Mr Geoff Hedges • Mr Geoff Killick
Mr F. Larkin • Mr Peter Lead • A.J. McConnel Esq.
Mr and Mrs L. Ockenden • Mrs M. Oliphant • Mr Will Thomas
Mr Graham Tubb • Mrs B. White • Mrs M. Wilkie
Mr and Mrs A. Williamson • Mrs Doreen Wright
Seaford Museum of Local History

BRITAIN IN OLD PHOTOGRAPHS

To order any of these titles please telephone Littlehampton Book Services on 01903 721596